Angela,

We are living beyond our spiritual means if we expect ourselves to honor in others that which we cannot honor in ourselves. May you begin to know & embrace all the intricate parts of yourself. Thank you for being in my life & allowing me to be a part of your life.

God Bless,
Robin S.
12/26/02

GARDEN
Psalms

Presented to:

_____

Presented by:

_____

Date:

_____

GARDEN
Psalms

*God's Gift
of Comfort
and Abundance*

Honor Books
Tulsa, Oklahoma

Garden Psalms
ISBN 1-56292-803-1

Copyright © 1999 by GRQ Ink, Inc.
381 Riverside Drive, Suite #250
Franklin, TN 37064

Published by Honor Books
P.O. Box 55388
Tulsa, OK 74155

Developed by GRQ Ink, Inc.
Manuscript written by Margaret Langstaff
Cover and text designed by Richmond & Williams
Composition by John Reinhardt Book Design

You open your hand,
satisfying the desire of every
living thing.

PSALM 145:16 NRSV

CREATION REVEALS THE WORK OF GOD

*The heavens keep telling the wonders of God,
and the skies declare what he has done.*

PSALM 19:1 CEV

❧

A clear, starry night in the country, away from city lights and noise, is the perfect way to clear your mind and put life's worries and frustrations in perspective. You might try counting the stars with your finger or picking out familiar constellations or searching for the North Star—or maybe, if you are lucky, catching a glimpse of a shooting star. The inky black sky, pierced by pinpricks of silver and gold, is breathtaking.

Phillip W. Keller in *A Shepherd Looks at Psalm 23* said, "I frequently go out at night to walk alone under the stars and remind myself of His majesty and might. Looking up at the star-studded sky I remember that at least 250,000,000 x 250,000,000 such bodies— each larger than our sun, one of the smallest of the stars—have been scattered across the vast spaces of the universe by His hand."

Look up to the heavens, and praise Him, our Lord, Creator of the universe. Rest in the assurance that His might is sufficient for us to overcome whatever troubles come our way.

O Lord, our Sovereign,
how majestic is thy name in all
the earth!

PSALM 8:9 NRSV

When I look at the night sky
and see the work of your fingers—
the moon and the stars you have set in place—
what are mortals that you should think of us,
mere humans that you should care for us?

PSALM 8:3–4 NLT

Your word, O Lord, is eternal;
it stands firm in the heavens.

PSALM 119:89 NIV

He counts the stars
and names each one.
Our Lord is great and very powerful.
There is no limit to what he knows.

PSALM 147:4–5 NCV

THIRST FOR GOD AND HIS PEACE

As a deer longs for flowing streams,
so my soul longs for you, O God.

PSALM 42:1 NRSV

A deer will not stop and drop its head to drink unless it feels perfectly secure. The situation must be quiet and still with no scent of a predator on the wind and no noise in the forest or stream. Only then will a deer drop its guard, expose its neck, and drink refreshing

water. Water is vital to the deer in another way besides drinking. When chased, a deer can escape harm only by using a stream or body of water to cover its tracks. A pursued deer looks frantically for water to save its life.

Take a moment to reflect on our kinship with the deer as one of God's creatures. The deer's desire for the safety of water is akin to our deep longing for God.

God gave us the gift of life, and He will preserve and protect us. We thirst for Him as a deer thirsts for water because without Him we cannot live in peace and security. In Him we are safe.

He maketh me to lie down in green pastures:
he leadeth me beside the still waters.
He restoreth my soul:
he leadeth me in the paths
of righteousness for his name's sake.
PSALM 23:2–3 KJV

GOD'S ABUNDANT PROVISION

Thou visiteth the earth, and waterest it:
thou greatly enrichest it with the river of God,
which is full of water.

PSALM 65:9 KJV

༄

Water is necessary for life.

A woman wanted to visit her daughter who had just given birth to her first child. The woman was a careful person who attended to every detail of her household, garden, and life. Because her husband was away on a business trip, she arranged for her handyman, a simple fellow, to look after everything while she was gone. She wrote down instructions and made sure the man fully understood.

She had a good time with her daughter and new grandchild and returned home a week later. When she unlocked the door, however, she noticed a wilted plant in the foyer. She walked on, miffed, to the kitchen, where she noticed full bowls of dog and cat food. Alarmed, she went searching for her pets. She found the dog and cat stretched out nearly dead, in the bathroom. Shaken, she realized she had forgotten to put "water" in her instructions.

Fortunately for us, God never forgets and always provides what we need. Do we languish out of a lack of understanding of God's care for us, or do we radiate quiet assurance and confidence in God's promise to provide for our daily needs?

The LORD is my shepherd, I shall
not want.
PSALM 23:1 NRSV

If you belong to the Lord, reverence him;
for everyone who does this has everything he needs.
Even strong young lions sometimes go hungry,
but those of us who reverence the Lord
will never lack any good thing.
PSALM 34:9-10 TLB

We praise you, Lord God!
You treat us with kindness
day after day,
and you rescue us.
You always protect us
and save us from death.
PSALM 68:19-20 CEV

I was crying to the LORD with my voice,
and He answered me from His holy mountain.
PSALM 3:4 NAS

Oh, thank GOD—he's so good!
His love never runs out.
PSALM 107:1 THE MESSAGE

LOOK TO GOD FOR PEACE AND REFRESHMENT IN TOUGH TIMES

*I reach out for you. I thirst for you
as parched land thirsts for rain.*

PSALM 143:6 TLB

In July and August 1988, certain counties in middle Tennessee experienced a drought. Despite the relentless midsummer heat—often at temperatures over 100 degrees—clouds were few and far between and the only moisture the ground had came from early morning dew. Cracks and fissures opened in the earth and grew wider and more frightening as the drought went on. The clay soil became like sandstone, hard and brittle, and eventually turned to dust. Water rationing was imposed. Gardens and fields burned to a crisp. Dead birds floated in livestock water tanks, having drowned trying to find water. Thirsty wild animals became bold and appeared in backyards and on front porches. People despaired of getting anything to grow that year, and farmers stopped planting and cultivating.

Only in early autumn did the drought break. The seasonal fall rains brought the land back from the brink of destruction and restored the water tables vital to the following year's sowing.

The land needed water like we need God. Without Him we languish and die. Do we turn to Him, the refreshing spring of our existence, often during the day and drink deeply?

The Law of the LORD
makes them happy,
and they think about it day and night.
They are like trees
growing beside a stream,
trees that produce fruit in season
and always have leaves.
Those people succeed in everything they do.

PSALM 1:2-3 CEV

What I want from you is your true thanks;
I want your promises fulfilled.
I want you to trust me in your times of trouble,
so I can rescue you, and you can give me glory.

PSALM 50:14-15 TLB

Those who are planted in the house of the LORD
Shall flourish in the courts of our God.
They shall still bear fruit in old age;
They shall be fresh and flourishing.

PSALM 92:13-14 NKJV

THE RIGHTEOUS SHALL FLOURISH

He shall come down like rain
upon the grass before mowing,
Like showers that water the earth.

PSALM 72:6 NKJV

∽

The wonderful odor of freshly cut grass, rich and clean smelling, is loved the world over by gardeners. Add to that the fresh scent that arises from lawns and fields when gentle summer showers fall on top of the mown blades. The sheer pleasure of it overwhelms the senses.

God's love, freely given, pours down on us gently all day, every day. He wants us to grow by it, find fulfillment in Him, and lead productive and abundant lives. He desires for us to develop our inner talents, the gifts that He Himself gave us, and make use of them in the world He created. He wants us to flourish in contentment and peace in the place where He has planted us.

Are we unaware of our daily provision from God, or do we stir and quicken with grace that is ours daily? Are we dissatisfied with our present life, or do we flower with the spiritual fulfillment that is a tribute to God and an inspiration to others? Let God's love pour down on you today; let Him shower your life with His good gifts.

In his days shall the righteous flourish;
and abundance of peace
so long as the moon endureth.

PSALM 72:7 KJV

There shall be an handful of corn
in the earth upon the top
of the mountains;
the fruit thereof shall shake
like Lebanon:
and they of the city shall flourish
like grass of the earth.

PSALM 72:16 KJV

You answer us with awesome
deeds of righteousness,
O God our Savior,
the hope of all the ends of the earth.

PSALM 65:5 KJV

Our Help Is in the Name of the Lord

Our help is in the name of the Lord,
who made heaven and earth.

PSALM 124:8 KJV

❧

Early this century one hundred scholars and preachers attended a seminar on prayer. They came from around the world, and most had impressive academic credentials and resumes that ran many pages. Over many days, prayer was discussed in great detail from all angles. At the close of the seminar, the final session was titled "Sincerity in Prayer." The participants wanted to discuss how to pray "authentically." After hours of windy discussion, an elderly gentleman stood up in the back of the room. He had led a life of quiet contemplation and gardening in the hills of Kentucky, and he was unaccustomed to speaking to crowds. But he rose to his feet, cleared his voice, and said, "Help me, Jesus." You could have heard a pin drop. What on earth did he mean? "Help me, Jesus," he continued in a soft voice, "is the prayer that always works for me."

Instead of approaching God in prayer through eloquent words, seek Him with a yielded and tender heart. Don't be afraid to call on God when you need Him. Rest in His strength and protection.

I will lift up my eyes to the hills—
From whence comes my help?
My help comes from the LORD,
Who made heaven and earth.
He will not allow your foot to be moved;
He who keeps you will not slumber.

PSALM 121:1–3 NKJV

GOD KEEPS HIS PROMISES—SO SHOULD WE

He gives food to those who fear him.
He remembers his agreement forever.

PSALM 111:5 NCV

Planting a garden is a commitment, as any gardener knows. The first seed set in the ground and covered with dirt is an oath all by itself. It is a beginning that will demand attention over a period of days, weeks, and months. Water, fertilizer, and weeding can only be supplied by the gardener at the right time and in the right amounts. And this means work. Planting is making a promise to care for the life we have started.

"He remembers his agreement forever" means God keeps His promises to us, promises that He has made because He has given us life and cares for us deeply. He will nurture us because He wants us to flourish. We all have our own individual place in His garden and are intended to be useful and a cause of great joy to Him.

Like God, our word should be our bond. Once you have made a promise, fulfill it joyfully and with thanks, remembering that the Lord is unswerving in His commitment to us.

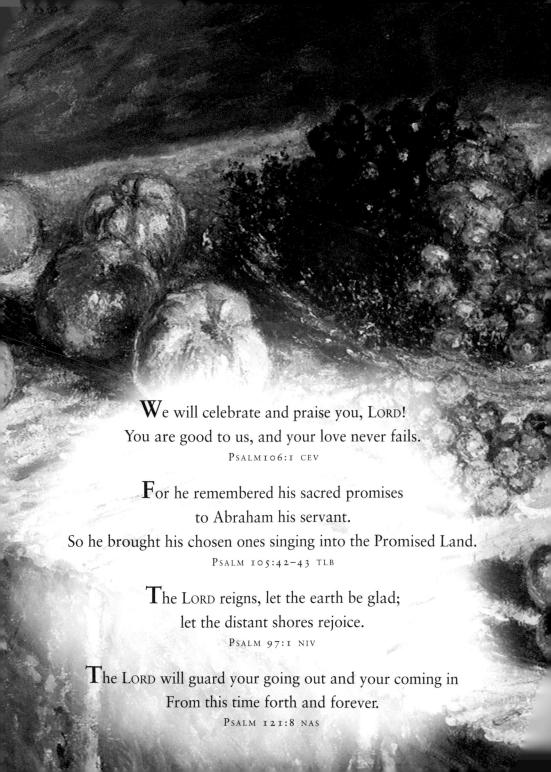

We will celebrate and praise you, Lord!
You are good to us, and your love never fails.

PSALM 106:1 CEV

For he remembered his sacred promises
to Abraham his servant.
So he brought his chosen ones singing into the Promised Land.

PSALM 105:42–43 TLB

The Lord reigns, let the earth be glad;
let the distant shores rejoice.

PSALM 97:1 NIV

The Lord will guard your going out and your coming in
From this time forth and forever.

PSALM 121:8 NAS

God's Creation Is Satisfied

He watereth the hills from his chambers:
the earth is satisfied with the fruit of thy works.

PSALM 104:13 KJV

The ancient motto of the Benedictine order is, "To pray is to work, to work is to pray." This is so entwined in the minds of the monks that the activities merge and become one and the same. God is present in everything they do, and their lives are hymns of praise and thanks to the Lord.

The Benedictines are great gardeners and go about their daily gardening tasks energized by the Spirit of God and desiring to make all they do worthy of His blessings. Their lives are satisfied with harmony and balance as they serve God in all things.

We are integral parts of God's plan for the world, His garden. God has given us everything we need to be satisfied with our place in life and to do good work in His name.

Pray for a keener awareness of this truth. Pray it lodges in your heart like a seed and brings forth roses of joy and usefulness, pleasing in the eyes of our Lord.

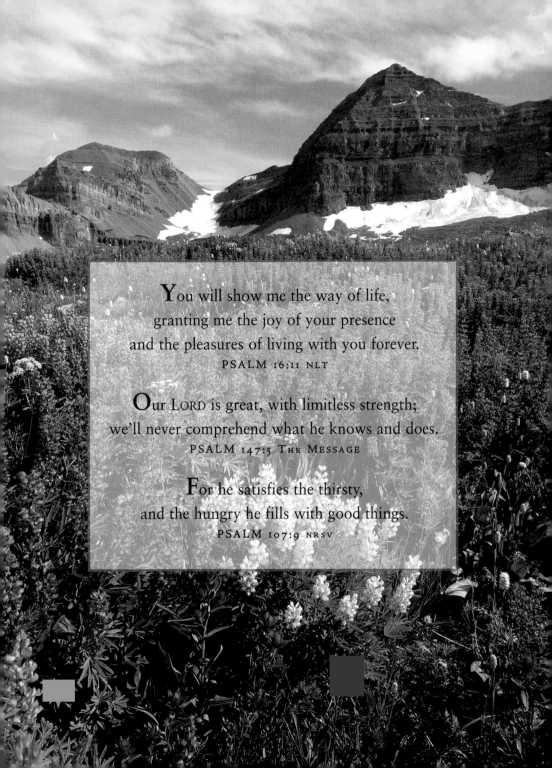

You will show me the way of life,
granting me the joy of your presence
and the pleasures of living with you forever.
PSALM 16:11 NLT

Our LORD is great, with limitless strength;
we'll never comprehend what he knows and does.
PSALM 147:5 THE MESSAGE

For he satisfies the thirsty,
and the hungry he fills with good things.
PSALM 107:9 NRSV

WE ARE GOD'S CREATION, AND WE OWE OUR LIVES TO HIM

Know that the LORD is God.
It is he that made us, and we are his;
we are his people, and the sheep of his pasture.

PSALM 100:3 NRSV

∾

Nothing is more satisfying to us as gardeners than to step back after a good day's work in the garden and survey a prospering bed of plants, which is directly a result of hours of planning and hard work. The beauty and fruitfulness of the plants are in direct proportion to

the amount of care and energy that have been devoted to them.

The garden with its perennials, annuals, vegetables, and fruits exists because we have established it, watched over it tenderly, and given it what it needs to grow.

This pleasurable experience gives us a small inkling of what it must be like for our Lord to survey the work of His hands. Our loving, diligent care for our gardens is a tiny mirror image of the love and care He lavishes on His creation. We belong to Him, we are His sheep, and He will do whatever is necessary to preserve and protect us.

Our responsibility in this equation is to flourish and grow in the knowledge that we are beloved of the Lord. Are we making the most of what He has given us?

So we Thy people
and the sheep of Thy pasture
Will give thanks to Thee forever;
To all generations we will tell of
Thy praise.

Psalm 79:13 NAS

A Long Life of Blessings with God

*The righteous flourish
like the palm tree,
and grow like a cedar in
Lebanon.*

Psalm 92:12 nrsv

The majestic cedar and palm trees were important to the people of the Bible. The cedar was used in ceremonial cleansing, in building, and for gifts. In the Bible the cedar is used figuratively for Israel's glory, Christ's glory, the growth of saints, and mighty nations. The palm tree was a site for judgeship; its fruit was used for food; its branches were used for roofing and shelter. It symbolized righteousness, beauty, and victory.

David knew his audience had all of these references for the two trees in their minds. When he said the righteous shall flourish like these two trees, he was saying that they would rise above others, become strong and revered in their eyes. He meant that by observing God's commandments and living lives of joyous faith, the righteous would be "right" with God and reap unimaginable blessings.

Do we love God? Do we obey His Word? Very simply, it is all God asks of us, and He asks this so we may grow and come into the many blessings He has prepared for us.

He has made His wonders to be remembered;
The LORD is gracious and compassionate.
He has given food to those who fear Him;
He will remember His covenant forever.

PSALM 111:4–5 NAS

Learn to Live in God's Time, Not Ours

But a thousand years mean nothing to you!
They are merely a day gone by
or a few hours in the night.

Digging in the earth, the gardener often comes across artifacts and evidence of days gone by. Arrowheads, horseshoes, belt buckles, pieces of pottery, and old bones sometimes are unearthed. We pause, holding them up to the light, and for a moment it becomes very clear to us that this particular day that we are spending in the sunshine on our knees in the garden will soon be one of our "yesterdays" and a faded memory. Yet we live in eternity when we rest in God. For He always was, always is, and always will be. As He said to Moses: "I am who I am" (Exodus 3:14 NKJV). There is no past, present, or future for the Creator of the universe. He simply "is." There are no seasons in God's "life," no cycles, no inclement weather. In fact, God does not "live" life, according to our understanding of the Word. He is life.

Take pleasure in the Father's unchanging love for you. Although many seasons will come and go throughout your life, find comfort in His sustaining and steadfast grace.

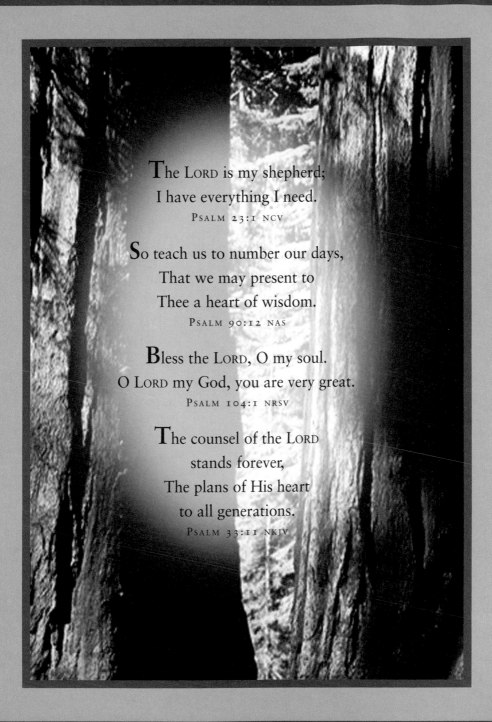

The LORD is my shepherd;
I have everything I need.
PSALM 23:1 NCV

So teach us to number our days,
That we may present to
Thee a heart of wisdom.
PSALM 90:12 NAS

Bless the LORD, O my soul.
O LORD my God, you are very great.
PSALM 104:1 NRSV

The counsel of the LORD
stands forever,
The plans of His heart
to all generations.
PSALM 33:11 NKJV

GOD, THE REFRESHMENT OF OUR LIVES

Singers and dancers alike say,
"All my springs are in you."

PSALM 87:7 NRSV

Singers and dancers played a large role in celebrations and worship during the period in which the Psalms were written. While dancers were not used in Temple functions, they accompanied singers and musicians in all kinds of social events and festivals. Singers and dancers were considered creative individuals and essential parts of communal events.

In this verse the psalmist is saying that the singers and dancers knew their source of inspiration and creativity was in God. The "springs" they speak of are the springs of inspiration and insight, the place where their creative "waters" originate.

Gardeners know that spring-fed creeks and waterways are pure and clean. The water does not dry up or run out. The land is refreshed from a spring. To have a spring on one's property is a cause for comfort, for one knows that water will always be plentiful.

Remember the strength that is ours in having God as our spring of living water, the source of all life and growth. He is always there, refreshing us with grace and inspiring us to new heights of creativity.

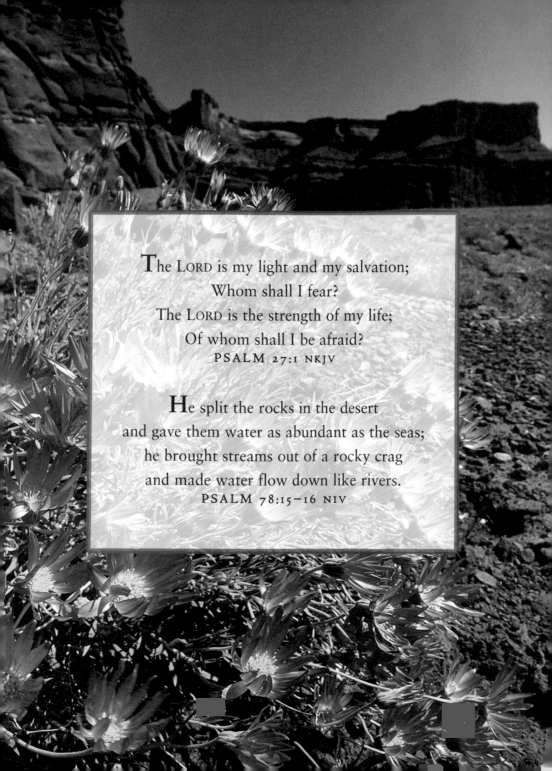

The LORD is my light and my salvation;
Whom shall I fear?
The LORD is the strength of my life;
Of whom shall I be afraid?
PSALM 27:1 NKJV

He split the rocks in the desert
and gave them water as abundant as the seas;
he brought streams out of a rocky crag
and made water flow down like rivers.
PSALM 78:15–16 NIV

GOD'S DELIVERANCE IN HIS ACCEPTABLE TIME

But as for me, my prayer is to you, O LORD.
At an acceptable time, O God,
in the abundance of your
steadfast love, answer me.

PSALM 69:13 NRSV

❧

A good part of a gardener's time involves waiting, and a big part of what we are waiting for is completely out of our control. We plant our seeds and set out seedlings. We know they should grow and produce within a certain period of time, but we can't be certain exactly when. We water and fertilize and weed and pray. We watch the weather forecasts hoping for favorable reports, but know that wind, hail, drought, and floods are always possibilities.

Uncertainty, then, is an unavoidable fact of a gardener's life. We can't hurry nature's pace just because we are impatient, and we can't predict what calamities, which are completely out of our hands, might befall our garden. We have to do all we can, then "keep the faith" and wait for the outcome.

The gardener's situation is very similar to our relationship with the Lord. God in His steadfast love for us hears all of our cries for help. He knows far better than we do when and how to answer us, so trust in His perfect timing.

Depend on the LORD;
trust him, and he will
take care of you.
Wait and trust the LORD.
Don't be upset when others get rich
or when someone else's plans succeed.
Don't get angry.
Don't be upset; it only leads to trouble.

PSALM 37:5,7–8 NCV

I waited patiently for the LORD;
and he inclined unto me, and heard my cry.

PSALM 40:1 KJV

Our LORD, we belong to you.
We tell you what worries us,
and you won't let us fall.

PSALM 55:22 CEV

SECURITY AND REST FOR THE SOUL

I will both lie down in peace, and sleep;
For You alone, O LORD, make me dwell in safety.

PSALM 4:8 NKJV

❦

It is morning in the garden. The gardener sips her coffee and checks to make sure she has all she needs: trowel, spade, hoe, hand fork, kneepad, and garden gloves. The sun has just dried the dew from the leaves of the young plants. There is much to be done; a full day lies ahead. The gardener looks forward to the work and the wonderful feeling of bone-tiredness awaiting her at the end of the day. The sweet satisfaction that comes from having accomplished what she set out to do. The contentment of mind and muscle that comes from a day of physical exertion. Will she ever sleep well that night!

Only too often worries mar our sleep. We toss and turn and check the clock and meet the morning exhausted. Anxiety and frustration are the enemies of a healthful rest.

❦

Lord, teach us the wisdom of doing all we can and then turning the rest of it over to You. Help us recognize that You are with us, day and night, and that we can truly relax and rest in that security.

I lay down and slept;
I awoke, for the LORD sustains me.

PSALM 3:5 NAS

But I call to God, and the LORD saves me.
Evening, morning and noon I cry out in distress,
and he hears my voice.

PSALM 55:16–17 NIV

And when I was burdened with worries,
you comforted me and made me feel secure.

PSALM 94:19 CEV

God is our refuge and strength,
a very present help in trouble.

PSALM 46:1 NRSV

The LORD is in His holy temple;
the LORD's throne is in heaven.
His eyes behold, His eyes test the sons of men.

PSALM 11:4 NAS

GOD'S PRESERVATION

Love the Lord, all you his saints.
The Lord preserves the faithful,
but abundantly repays the one who acts haughtily.

PSALM 31:23 NRSV

❧

Sometimes when we are at work in the garden it's easy to imagine we are "playing god" with our seeds and plants. We move them around, decide which needs water or fertilizer. We dispatch haughty, upstart weeds mercilessly and slaughter whole nations of bugs. Our job is to protect the garden and do what is necessary for the plants to flourish. If a plant is a good one and is behaving itself, it gets love and attention. It gets to live.

It is also the gardener's responsibility to make life-and-death decisions about the garden. If we let everything run rampant, the garden would turn to chaos and weeds. Each plant has a place and a purpose.

In much the same way, God plants and cultivates us. He knows what we can become, if only we will be faithful. If we honor His love with our obedience, we will grow and flourish.

We must look at ourselves carefully and ask if we are faithful. Are we responding to the care and mercy God lavishes on us by growing and bearing fruit as He intended?

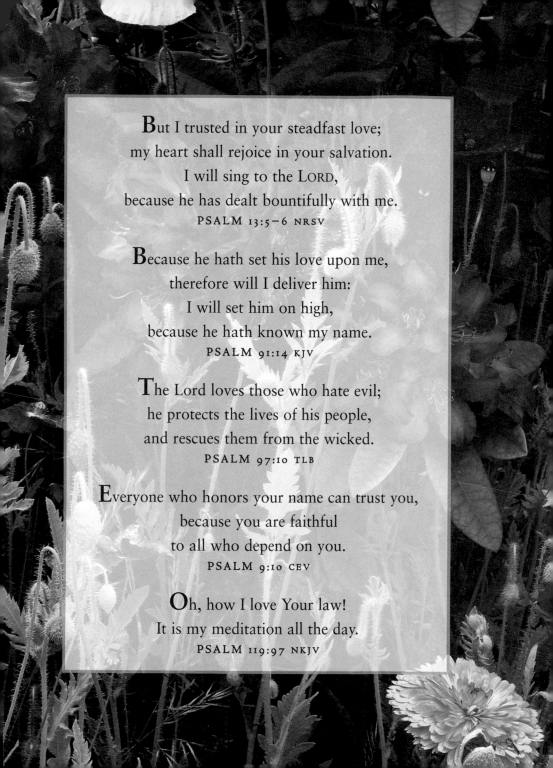

But I trusted in your steadfast love;
my heart shall rejoice in your salvation.
I will sing to the LORD,
because he has dealt bountifully with me.

PSALM 13:5–6 NRSV

Because he hath set his love upon me,
therefore will I deliver him:
I will set him on high,
because he hath known my name.

PSALM 91:14 KJV

The Lord loves those who hate evil;
he protects the lives of his people,
and rescues them from the wicked.

PSALM 97:10 TLB

Everyone who honors your name can trust you,
because you are faithful
to all who depend on you.

PSALM 9:10 CEV

Oh, how I love Your law!
It is my meditation all the day.

PSALM 119:97 NKJV

I Bend but Don't Break in Troubled Times

But I am like a green olive tree
in the house of God.
I trust in the steadfast love of God forever and ever.

Psalm 52:8 nrsv

❧

Olive trees have been a key resource and bounty to mankind for many generations. The luscious oil from this tree has been commonly used in cooking and skin-care products. It is also known for its cleansing benefits to the liver and has been used in temple rituals.

Though comparable to the size of an apple tree, the olive tree takes fifteen years to mature and bear fruit and is capable of living for hundreds of years. Yet unlike the typical aged tree, it is flexible and adaptable, and thus, full of the promised bounty of which David speaks in the Scripture above.

In this verse David describes his own life as full of promise because of his unwavering trust "in the steadfast love of God" and "in the house of God." David's sublime joy was in his Creator, who had given him the qualities necessary for surviving whatever came his way.

Look to the Lord. Place your reliance upon Him. Let Him guide and direct you daily so that you may also thrive and prosper.

I will be glad and rejoice in your love,
for you saw my affliction
and knew the anguish of my soul.

PSALM 31:7 NIV

How blessed is the man
who has made the LORD his trust,
And has not turned to
the proud, nor to those
who lapse into falsehood.

PSALM 40:4 NAS

Return, O my soul, to your rest,
for the LORD has dealt
bountifully with you.

PSALM 116:7 NRSV

Though the LORD is supreme,
he takes care of those who are humble,
but he stays away from the proud.

PSALM 138:6 NCV

GOD IS MY PORTION
AND THE SOURCE OF ALL MY GROWTH

Whom have I in heaven but you?
And there is nothing on earth
that I desire other than you.

PSALM 73:25 NRSV

Sunflowers are one of the most dazzling
gifts of the summer garden. Large and
imposing, they majestically climb higher
and higher above all other flowers until they tower over the entire
garden. By degrees they then unfold splendid discs of yellow petals
with a wealth of tightly packed seeds in their center—seeds that will
one day feed birds, animals, and people, and will produce hundreds
more sunflower plants.

The sunflower's love for the sun consumes its entire being. After
growing tall enough to be free of the threat of any shade, its face
follows the course of the sun throughout the day, leaning and turning
in the direction of the sun's circuit. More than any other plant, the
sunflower seeks to be at all times fully bathed in sunlight.

We need God the way the sunflower needs the sun. Seek Him
first every morning. Pray throughout the day to always keep your
heart focused in His direction.

Let me hear of your steadfast
love in the morning,
for in you I put my trust.
Teach me the way I should go,
for to you I lift up my soul.

PSALM 143:8 NRSV

GOD WILL PROVIDE FOR ALL OUR NEEDS

The day is thine,
the night also is thine:
thou has prepared the light and the sun.

PSALM 74:16 KJV

∽

Gardeners are keenly aware of the quality and duration of light throughout the growing season. The first short, cool spring days with their mild light gradually lengthen over the course of the season into the warm, rich, light-soaked days of summer that seem almost never ending. Daylight savings time comes and outdoor activities are at their height. Late in August the quality of the light mellows and the days grow shorter.

The psalmist acknowledges God's control over the source of the time-marking changes in light. The day in which we live and work belongs to Him, as does the night in which we go about our evening routines and rituals. God, as the Master of the universe, created the stars and planets and our sun. The Lord has complete control over the length and quality of our days and nights.

By acknowledging the Lord's control over all our hours, we gain the grace needed to lead full and productive lives. We enter into the presence and power of God.

For a day in Thy courts is better than a
thousand outside.
I would rather stand at the
threshold of the house of my God,
Than dwell in the tents of wickedness.

PSALM 84:10 NAS

He who dwells in the shelter of the Most High
will rest in the shadow of the Almighty.

PSALM 91:1 NIV

The LORD is your keeper;
the LORD is your shade at your right hand.
The sun shall not strike you by day,
nor the moon by night.

PSALM 121:5–6 NRSV

REWARD FOR RIGHTEOUS LIVING

For the LORD God is a sun and shield;
he bestows favor and honor.
No good thing does the LORD withhold
from those who walk uprightly.

❧

In the nineteenth-century home garden, gardeners often put up windbreaks in the form of tall, solid fencing to protect their plants from strong, cold winds and thus extend the growing season. There in the sunniest spot near the house, protected from ill winds, the gardeners would sow the kitchen vegetables, herbs, and spices they depended on for their meals. In that privileged preserve, the sun could do its work uninterrupted by unruly, unpredictable weather.

Today's gardeners use similar stratagems to protect and preserve the fruits of their labor: privacy fences and pest barriers; netting to hold seeds in place; weed-blocking materials, mulch, and cages to support fragile plants. The healthy plants, those that respond to the care lavished upon them, receive even more attention. The rest are rooted out.

In the same way, God preserves and protects the lives of those committed to Him, the lives surrendered to His protection and cultivation. He desires them to reach a bountiful harvest.

IN You, O LORD, I put my trust;
Let me never be ashamed;
Deliver me in Your righteousness.

PSALM 31:1 NKJV

GOD PROVIDES FOR ALL HIS CREATION— MAN AND BEAST

He giveth to the beast his food, and
to the young ravens which cry.

PSALM 147:9 KJV

Spring brings with it baby birds . . . and their busy parents. Gardeners are accompanied by lots of bird activity while they are outdoors about their tasks. From the earliest stirrings of spring, the birds are in evidence, singing and crying from tree limbs for mates, zooming around picking up material for nests, and making nests just about anywhere that seems safe to lay eggs and raise a family. Their tireless devotion to this work is marvelous to watch. And when the eggs hatch, the bird parents only redouble their efforts. For their

part, the little ones, when not eating, only scream louder for more. Their outsize mouths are open with hunger and desire, and their eyes are squeezed shut in earnestness. Their demanding din fills the air. These helpless receptacles of food require constant attention and protection from Mom and Dad.

God's hand is in this mystery, for He established it and set it on His course. The Lord loves all of His creation, and He provides for them all.

Let the heavens be glad, and let the earth rejoice!
Let the sea and everything in it shout his praise!
Let the fields and their crops burst forth with joy!
Let the trees of the forest rustle with praise!

PSALM 96:11–12 NLT

God Gives Strength to My Soul
as I Seek Him

When I asked for your help,
you answered my prayer and gave me courage.

Psalm 138:3 cev

❧

No matter how experienced we are as gardeners, questions arise. There are new plants we want to try or the lilies seem to be having a hard time of it this year or for some reason the tomatoes are not doing so well. Once the problem is recognized, we search for answers. We ask knowledgeable people or friends who are gardeners, we go to the library, or we call the county agricultural agent. And though we might not discover the answer immediately, the fact that we are doing something about it confers a sense of peace and determination. We know that eventually we will run down the answer. This is because we know what we need and where to find it. Sources are out there. All we have to do is narrow them down to the right one.

Knowing we need God's help and calling upon Him are the sureties that He indeed will answer us. It gives us the instant shot of strength we need for our journey.

The LORD shall preserve thy going out
and thy coming in from this time forth,
and even for evermore.
PSALM 121:8 KJV

He renews my strength.
He guides me along right paths,
bringing honor to his name.
PSALM 23:3 NLT

In my distress I cried to the LORD,
And He heard me.
PSALM 120:1 NKJV

I will pray to the LORD,
and he will answer me from his holy mountain.
PSALM 3:4 NCV

I go to bed and sleep in peace,
because, LORD, only you keep me safe.
PSALM 4:8 NCV

All Creation Is God's, and Nothing Surprises Him

The heavens are thine, the earth also is thine:
as for the world and the fulness thereof,
thou hast founded them.

Psalm 89:11 KJV

Our lives as gardeners are filled with wonder and surprise. Although we go about our tasks and duties in a kind of routine, methodical way, each day brings something unexpected. Sometimes the wonder and surprise are so great, we are knocked back and simply overwhelmed. We lift a rock in a remote part of the garden and find a garter snake staring back at us. We catch a glimpse of a bed of zinnias in the full light of a summer afternoon and the colors and vigor of what God has wrought renders us speechless. Or, on a less pleasant note, we discover that overnight the deer have trampled the vegetables.

Whether their cause is good or bad, surprise and wonder thread their way through each day we garden. Our hours are full of mystery and discovery and often feelings of helplessness.

We can rest assured that God is neither surprised by our trials and tribulations nor unable to help us overcome anything thrown in our way.

O Lord my God, many and many a time
you have done great miracles for us
and we are ever in your thoughts.
Who else can do such glorious things?
No one else can be compared with you.
There isn't time to tell
of all your wonderful deeds.

PSALM 40:5 TLB

GOD'S BLESSINGS ON FAMILIES

Your wife will be like a fruitful vine
within your house;
your children will be like olive shoots
around your table.

PSALM 128:3 NRSV

In this verse David used images his rural listeners would readily understand. They would be able to translate easily the spiritual message embedded in them. Most of his people were farmers and gardeners. Grapes and olives were important crops to them. They, in addition to grain, made up the basis of the people's diet. They were plants people planted and cultivated with their sweat and toil and harvested for their families to eat at their tables. They were the sustenance that supported their lives. These people understood clearly that David was saying that the man who gives his life over to God and keeps His commandments will, according to God's promise, be blessed by God. He will be surrounded with abundance. He will have love and joy within the walls of his home. He will be a source of inspiration and growth to others.

God's promises are unfailing. If we attend to His Word and keep to the path He has shown us, He will reward our faithfulness and devotion with gifts beyond our wildest imagination.

Unless the Lord builds a house,
the builders' work is useless.
Unless the Lord protects a city,
sentries do no good.

PSALM 127:1 TLB

The Glory of God in Creation

O LORD, our Lord,
How excellent is Your name in all the earth,
Who have set Your glory above the heavens!

PSALM 8:1 NKJV

Red-tailed hawks are a familiar but fascinating sight to gardeners. They seem to swim in a pool of blue overhead, lordly dominating the scene from on high. The view from their altitude must make the rest of life seem puny. They seem so serene and above it all—impossibly high, beautiful, and remote. For a moment we may catch ourselves daydreaming about what it might be like to soar above the earth as they do, peering down on the glorious green earth teeming with life. At times like these we let go of our worries and cares, forget what we are doing, and become totally absorbed in the glory and wonder of the moment. We are lifted out of ourselves and caught up in the miracle of life. Afterward, we inevitably fall back to pondering the utter beauty and surpassing grandeur of the world God has created.

God gives us these moments as gifts to refresh our spirits in Him. For seconds at a time He reveals Himself to us in ways we can absorb.

The LORD is far above
all of the nations;
he is more glorious
than the heavens.
PSALM 113:4 CEV

Praise ye the LORD.
Praise ye the LORD from the heavens:
praise him in the heights.
Praise ye him, all his angels:
praise ye him, all his hosts.
Praise ye him, sun and moon:
praise him, all ye starts of light.
Praise him, ye heavens of heavens,
and ye waters that be above
the heavens.
PSALM 148:1-4 KJV

OUR PROTECTION COMES FROM GOD

You hem me in, behind and before,
and lay your hand upon me.

PSALM 139:5 NRSV

～

All gardeners know that a beautiful garden doesn't just happen. It requires tender touching, careful seedling separation, expert deadheading of faded flowers, and timely pruning. Gardeners know that plants have to be watched over and gently attended to like small children in order to grow up safely. Plants have to be delicately prodded in the right direction and firmly protected from threat. They are like helpless babies that will suffer without watchful observation and intervention in times of trouble.

While in this verse David was using sheep as an analogy to make his point, it is an easy leap from pasture to garden in terms of what is needed in life to prosper— direct and constant development from the Caregiver.

———

It is in the daily discipline of looking to God, allowing Him to do the work needed in the smallest details of our lives, that we grow beautifully in His image.

He will not allow your foot to slip;
He who keeps you will not slumber.

PSALM 121:3 NAS

For the Lord watches over all the plans
and paths of godly men,
but the paths of the godless lead to doom.

PSALM 1:6 TLB

GOD KNOWS WHEN WE NEED REST

*He maketh me to lie down in
green pastures: he leadeth me
beside the still waters.
He restoreth my soul.*

PSALM 23:2–3 KJV

∽

Phillip W. Keller, in *A Shepherd Looks at Psalm 23*, did a masterful commentary on this psalm for the modern reader who is not versed in the ways of sheep or the difficult demands made upon the shepherd in caring for them. One point that Keller made over and over again is the sheer helplessness and distressing vulnerability of sheep. Domesticated sheep simply cannot take care of themselves at all. They have to be watched over with the most serious vigilance. The slightest oversight or the least bit of neglect can spell disaster for the flock. The sheep even have to be shown when and how to rest or they will completely wear themselves out and fall prey to disease and predators.

To gardeners, sheep would resemble the most fragile roses: susceptible to every whim of the weather, nothing more than dead sticks if not pampered to the utmost.

Do we have any inkling of how weak and helpless we are without God? Our Lord knows and protects us from everything, even ourselves, if we place our trust in Him.

Come, see the glorious things
God has done.
What marvelous miracles
happen to his people!
PSALM 66:5 TLB

I have set the LORD always before me;
Because He is at my right hand I shall not be moved.
Therefore my heart is glad, and my glory rejoices;
My flesh also will rest in hope.
PSALM 16:8–9 NKJV

Let me live with you forever and find protection
under your wings, my God.
You heard my promises,
and you have blessed me,
just as you bless everyone
who worships you.
PSALM 61:4–5 CEV

The LORD will guard you as you come and go,
both now and forever.
PSALM 121:8 NCV

ONLY GOD CAN SATISFY YOUR HUNGER
AND THIRST

O God, you are my God, I seek you,
my soul thirsts for you;
my flesh faints for you.

Have you ever run into a gardenaholic? Someone obsessed with his or her garden, gardening in general, or some species of plant, and who can't stop talking about it, running around to garden shows and nurseries, dominating garden club meetings? Someone who has gone over the edge with the passion for gardening? They exist, though they are fortunately in a minority. They are similar to other obsessive-compulsive types: workaholics, exercise addicts, shopaholics, and compulsive gamblers.

All of these people have one thing in common. They are confused about what they need. Trying to fill the emptiness in their hearts, they substitute counterfeits for the real thing. Trying to outrun their terrible sense of longing in the manic pursuit of phantom pleasures, they ultimately fail. You will notice they are never happy and always restless. To them, anything that takes them away from their obsession is a waste of time.

We are not to let anybody or anything be more important in our lives than God. Any other priority will eventually leave us unfulfilled.

I lift my hands to you in prayer.
As a dry land needs rain, I thirst for you.

PSALM 143:6 NCV

GOD'S BOUNTY TO THOSE
WHO KEEP HIS WAYS

There will be an abundance of grain in the earth,
On the top of the mountains;
Its fruit shall wave like Lebanon;
And those of the city shall flourish like grass
of the earth.

PSALM 72:16 NKJV

∽

The Old Farmer's Almanac 1999 contains a story entitled
"How to Live to Be 100." It discusses the Rhodope people of Bul-
garia who have the world's largest percentage of centenarians, 50 for
every 100,000 people (the United States has only 19 for every
100,000). A doctor who has studied them said, "They have one thing
in common. None of them wears a watch." And listen to a few of
these old-timers' own explanations for their longevity: "We take
natural food, work with the land and with the animals. I get up with
the sun. I have a clock, but I can't read it" (Minka Asenova Bendeva,
92); "I take care of myself" (Maria Chongarova, 103, who eats a
diet of goat cheese, homemade bread, olives, fruits,
and vegetables); and "God knows *His* job, and He
will give me whatever He pleases" (Shina
Anastsova Iancheva, 94, who shares her home
with five generations of her family).

Are we diligent in our daily lives to seek God's path at every
moment? Don't be distracted from doing His work through which
He will bless our lives beyond measure.

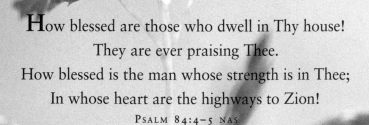

How blessed are those who dwell in Thy house!
They are ever praising Thee.
How blessed is the man whose strength is in Thee;
In whose heart are the highways to Zion!

PSALM 84:4–5 NAS

They eat the rich food in your house,
and you let them drink from your river of pleasure.
You are the giver of life.
Your light lets us enjoy life.

PSALM 36:8–9 NCV

You who have made me see many
troubles and calamities will revive me again;
from the depths of the earth you will bring me up again.
You will increase my honor, and comfort me once again.

PSALM 71:20–21 NRSV

POWER OF GOD

The waters saw thee, O God,
the waters saw thee; they were afraid:
the depths also were troubled.

PSALM 77:16 KJV

People tend to want to emphasize God's tender mercies and patient love. But that is only part of the story. If we exclude, because it makes us uncomfortable, His awesome power, we distort the

nature of the Lord and miss knowing Him as He is.

Gardeners know God is love, but nature reveals He is much more. Just as there is a soft breeze that causes flowers to sway in the sunlight, there is also the gale of the hurricane. The gentle rain waters our garden, but the flood erases all in its path. And there is the volcano, the tornado, the earthquake, and the avalanche. Just as God creates, He also, for the purpose of redemption, destroys.

When was the last time you considered God's power with awe, fear, and wonder?

I shall remember the deeds of the LORD;
Surely I will remember Thy wonders of old.
I will meditate on all Thy work,
And muse on Thy deeds.
Thy way, O God, is holy;
What god is great like our God?
Thou art the God who workest wonders;
Thou hast made known
Thy strength among the peoples.
Thou hast by Thy power redeemed Thy people.

PSALM 77:11-15 NAS

GOD IS OUR SOURCE FOR ALL THINGS

Protect me and save me because you are my God.
I am your faithful servant, and I trust you.

PSALM 86:2 CEV

⌘

A busy mother and housewife had little time for her garden, but tried to squeeze in stolen moments throughout her hectic days to cultivate her flowers and a tiny vegetable patch. She also kept gardenia bushes around the perimeter of her house because she loved their fragrance wafting in through the open windows. Gardening, for her, was a bit of time to be quiet and refreshed.

One spring morning, as she was finishing the dishes, she realized her youngest child was missing. After looking all over to no avail, she went outdoors, calling her. Finally, from around the corner of the house the little one appeared, smiling and holding her skirt out like a basket.

Fighting back tears, the mother scolded her. She then hugged her and offered a prayer of thanksgiving to God. As she did so, she noticed what her darling was carrying in her skirt: nearly a hundred tight, green gardenia buds.

⸻

Lord, Your ways are subtle and Your blessings often mixed. Sometimes You even seem to be teasing us. Teach us to be patient as You work Your will in our lives.

To you, O Lord, I lift up my soul.

PSALM 25:1 NRSV

Hear the voice of my
supplications when I cry to Thee for help,
When I lift up my hands
toward Thy holy sanctuary.

PSALM 28:2 NAS

For the Lord God is a sun and shield:
the Lord will give grace and glory:
no good thing will he withhold
from them that walk uprightly.

PSALM 84:11 KJV

THE SOVEREIGNTY AND PROVIDENCE OF GOD

Whatever the LORD pleases he does,
in heaven and on earth,
in the seas and all deeps.

PSALM 135:6 NRSV

At the age of sixteen a beautiful young girl was diagnosed with a rare and deadly form of cancer. The tragedy hit the family from out of the blue. Until this time the child had been in perfect health. Her parents and her brothers adored her.

The family attended church regularly, and the congregation rallied around them. The best medical care was obtained. Even so, after eighteen months of therapy in extreme discomfort, she passed away.

The parents were inconsolable. The father buried himself in his work. The mother withdrew and only puttered in her garden. Over a period of weeks she realized her puttering had developed a theme and a purpose. All of her plant choices had been pink and white, her daughter's favorite colors. So began a beautiful memorial that helped her heal her unspeakable pain: Katie's Garden.

The mysteries of life and death are not always disclosed to us. It is through persevering in faith that we realize the comfort of resting in the Father's loving wisdom. We can trust Him to carry us through life's greatest challenges and to turn our sorrows into joy.

Our Lord is great and very powerful.
There is no limit to what he knows.

PSALM 147:5 NCV

Lord, who may abide in Your tabernacle?
Who may dwell in Your holy hill?
He who walks uprightly,
And works righteousness,
And speaks the truth in his heart.

PSALM 15:1–2 NKJV

GOD CAN BE TRUSTED TO DELIVER OUR SOULS

But I trusted in your steadfast love;
my heart shall rejoice in your salvation.

PSALM 13:5 NRSV

Have you ever been wrongly accused of something? It's insulting, whether a policeman accuses you of speeding, your husband accuses you of borrowing and failing to return his handsaw, or a credit-card company accuses you of missing a payment. And it is even worse when circumstantial evidence points to you as the culprit. The policeman's radar went off when you went by, the last time your husband saw the handsaw it was in your hand, the credit-card company doesn't have your check so you obviously didn't send it. Talk about frustration!

What, they don't trust you? And why don't they believe what you're saying? You stomp out of the house and vigorously yank weeds out of the garden for an hour and gradually you feel a little better about the situation. The truth will win out, you are sure. Your innocence will be proven.

When our actions and thoughts are upright and entrusted to the Lord, we don't have to vindicate ourselves. We can rest assured in the fact that He will deliver us from any unjust situation. Our job is only to trust Him.

Your innocence will be clear to everyone.
He will vindicate you with the blazing light
of justice shining down as from the noonday sun.

PSALM 37:6 TLB

Lord, be good to those who are good,
whose hearts are honest.

PSALM 125:4 NCV

EACH ONE OF GOD'S CREATIONS IS UNIQUE

From the place of his habitation
he looketh upon all the inhabitants of the earth.
He fashioneth their hearts . . .
he considereth all their works.

PSALM 33:14–15 KJV

The buzzword these days is *biodiversity.* Scientists have stumbled on the amazing fact that variety in nature is important. The more species we have roving the earth, the healthier the planet will be.

Farmers discovered this a long time ago when they depleted their soil by growing a single crop in it for years at a time. In fact, our nation's push westward in the eighteenth and nineteenth centuries was propelled in large part by the soil erosion caused by planting cotton over and over again. The land had to be abandoned.

Intuitively the gardener asks, "Why on earth would anybody want to plant just one thing?" Variety is the spice of life. It's what makes a garden a garden, instead of just a bed of begonias. No two snowflakes are alike, nor are any two hearts.

Variety is pleasing to the Lord. Rejoice in the variety of people and circumstances God brings to your life; each will be a path of growth and maturity.

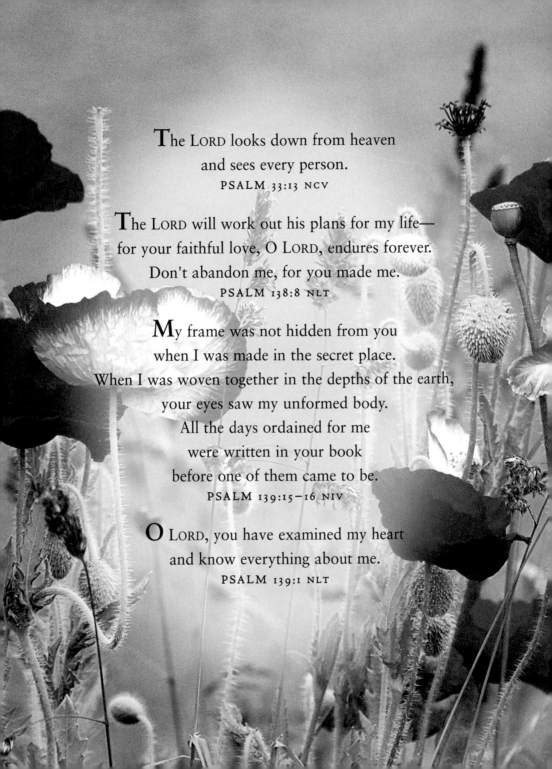

The Lord looks down from heaven
and sees every person.
PSALM 33:13 NCV

The Lord will work out his plans for my life—
for your faithful love, O Lord, endures forever.
Don't abandon me, for you made me.
PSALM 138:8 NLT

My frame was not hidden from you
when I was made in the secret place.
When I was woven together in the depths of the earth,
your eyes saw my unformed body.
All the days ordained for me
were written in your book
before one of them came to be.
PSALM 139:15–16 NIV

O Lord, you have examined my heart
and know everything about me.
PSALM 139:1 NLT

ONLY IN GOD ARE WE VICTORIOUS OVER SIN AND EVIL

*In God we have boasted continually,
and we will give thanks to your name forever.*

PSALM 44:8 NRSV

Boasting is bad manners, bad form, and bad style. What is David talking about here?

The Amish women, who are modest and plain both in their personal habits and in their homes, take great pride in their gardens. In her book about the Amish entitled *Plain and Simple*, Sue Bender said gardening is the one area in their lives where they really let themselves go. They plan gorgeous, sumptuous displays of color, and they group species of flowers for the greatest visual impact. Their gardens are showpieces and each one tries to out-wow the other. This is all right in their way of thinking because the garden comes from God. The glory is really His.

Every good thing comes from the Lord. Not only does He bless us with splendorous beauty in His creation and the love of family and friends, but He also protects us from harm and delivers us from evil and temptation.

Let us boast not in ourselves, but in the Lord. He made heaven and earth and all that is in it. Let's thank Him for our daily bread and praise Him for His mercy.

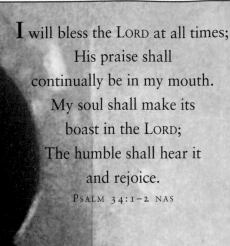

I will bless the Lord at all times;
His praise shall
continually be in my mouth.
My soul shall make its
boast in the Lord;
The humble shall hear it
and rejoice.

PSALM 34:1-2 NAS

Keep me safe, O God,
for in you I take refuge.
I said to the Lord, "You are my Lord;
apart from you I have no good thing."

PSALM 16:1-2 NIV

ABUNDANT BLESSINGS EVERY DAY

*Blessed be the Lord, who
daily bears our burden,
The God who is our salvation.*

∽

Each day has its own assortment of difficulties, which, while not necessarily earthshaking, may be just enough to sap our strength and wear on our nerves. For example: Japanese beetles are invading the garden; fine, you know how to get rid of them, but it means a trip to the store—fighting traffic both ways—and standing in line. Or, the onion sets have died before you had time to set them out; yes, you can get more, but you hadn't counted on paying for them twice. You're hoeing like mad and—*whop*—you chop yourself in the foot and it hurts. Your cellular phone rings while you're in the garden covered with dirt and straw: Little Billy has a fever and needs to be picked up from school. Life is one thing after another.

Our Lord is there not only in times of calamity. He is also with us in times of ordinary aggravation when our tempers grow short and our to–do lists grow long.

Let everyone bless God and sing his praises,
for he holds our lives in his hands.
And he holds our feet to the path.

<small>PSALM 66:8–9 TLB</small>

Then the earth will yield its harvest,
and God, our God, will richly bless us.

<small>PSALM 67:6 NLT</small>

Praise God, who did not ignore my prayer
or hold back his love from me.

<small>PSALM 66:20 NCV</small>

GOD WORKS MIRACLES

He opened the rock, and water gushed out;
it flowed through the desert like a river.

PSALM 105:41 NRSV

Fertilizer can work wonders. Getting just the right nutrients to plants at critical stages during their growth can make the difference between championship plants and mediocre flowers and vegetables. Fertilizer companies tout their products as miraculous potions that can transform ordinary plants into supernatural superstars. Gardening magazines have advertisements showing gardeners standing next to giant flowers and vegetables that have been dosed with these chemicals. The gardeners beam at the gigantic life forms they have cultivated, plants that dwarf the average vegetation. Pumpkins the size of Volkswagens, peaches the size of basketballs. "It's a miracle!" the ads say.

We close the magazines, inspired to achieve similar results—perhaps not as grotesque as the oversize vegetables, but outstanding nonetheless. We want "miraculous" plants too, though we know to call them such is only to use a figure of speech. God alone can work miracles because He stands outside nature, and indeed created nature.

Let us open our hearts to the miracle of God's saving grace so that He may work wonders with our lives, and we may become all that He would have us become.

Give thanks to the LORD, call on his name;
make known among the nations
what he has done.
Sing to him, sing praise to him;
tell of all his wonderful acts.

PSALM 105:1–2 NIV

GOODNESS FROM GOD

*I said to the LORD, "You are my Lord.
Every good thing I have comes from you."*

PSALM 16:2 NCV

☙

The Lord chose us, but we must also choose Him and draw close to Him.

An avid gardener used to suffer periods of depression in the winter. Friends told her to cheer up, and they did things to distract her. Her husband thought the whole thing was in her head because she missed being outdoors. None of this was very helpful. Try as she could, she could not pull herself out of these winter blues. She slept a lot and could barely drag herself around. This went on for many years.

Finally, she went to a doctor. He told her she was suffering from seasonal affective disorder caused by the dim winter light. He advised her to buy a special lamp and sit under it for fifteen minutes every morning. She did, and the results were dramatic.

She needed light just as much as her flowers did.

Like this woman and sunlight, we fade and flounder when we drift away from God. Recognizing this is the first step we must take to once again benefit from His blessings.

Oh how great is thy goodness,
which thou hast laid up for them that fear thee;
which thou hast wrought for them
that trust in thee before the sons of men!

PSALM 31:19 KJV

I will cry to the God of heaven
who does such wonders for me.

PSALM 57:2 TLB

Yes, the LORD will give what is good;
And our land will yield its increase.
Righteousness will go before Him,
And shall make His footsteps our pathway.

PSALM 85:12–13 NKJV

Do not fret because of the wicked;
do not be envious of wrongdoers,
for they will soon fade like the grass,
and wither like the green herb.

PSALM 37:1–2 NRSV

Our God is just.

Grass and herbs have shallow roots, as gardeners know. They can seem robust and strong, but in times of drought and cold weather they are among the first green things to succumb. In a very real sense, they have no firm foundation compared to perennials, shrubs, and trees, which are far more hardy and have deep, moisture-seeking roots. Grass and herbs are surface greenery, mere ground cover.

In comparing the wicked and wrongdoers to grass and herbs, David is saying that they may flourish for a short time, but not for long. The temporary prosperity of the wicked is a sour thing for us to contemplate, but we can be certain God will judge every man who has not walked according to His commandments nor placed his hope in Him.

We must not be downcast when the unrighteous seem to be doing better than we are. We should stick with God's plan for us and soldier on.

Arise, LORD! Lift up your hand, O God.
Do not forget the helpless.
Why does the wicked man revile God?
Why does he say to himself,
"He won't call me to account"?
But you, O God, do see trouble and grief.

PSALM 10:12–14 NIV

THE FACE OF GOD SHINES UPON US AND NOURISHES US

*Restore us, O God;
let your face shine, that we may be saved.*

PSALM 80:3 NRSV

Confidence is a wonderful thing. When we are confident in a particular area of our lives, we are at peace and at our highest level of productivity. Our confidence is usually the result of experience; we've done something so many times that we have learned to do it right and well. In the same way we can be confident in friends when we've relied on them so many times we know they'd never let us down. Confidence is the surety of a positive outcome.

Likewise, the best gardeners are those who over the years have tried and failed and tried again until they got it right. They've seen a lot of things come and go. They have amassed a wealth of information about plants, soil, and weather. They meet each spring with quiet excitement and a levelheaded confidence.

The more we call upon the Lord in our daily lives, the more peace and confidence we will have. And as we learn to rely completely on Him, the more we will realize that we can have total confidence in Him.

Commit your way to the LORD,
Trust also in Him,
And He shall bring it to pass.
He shall bring forth your righteousness as the light,
And your justice as the noonday.

PSALM 37:5–6 NKJV

It is better to trust the LORD
than to put confidence in people.
It is better to trust the LORD
than to put confidence in princes.

PSALM 118:8–9 NLT

Fear Nothing,
Including What you Can't See

You shall not be afraid of the terror by night,
Nor of the arrow that flies by day,
Nor of the pestilence that walks in darkness,
Nor of the destruction that lays waste at noonday.

PSALM 91:5-6 NRSV

Gardening would seem to be a tame and safe activity. And it usually is. Aphids are terrifying to look at under a microscope, but we can pinch their heads with our fingers. Moles, if they were ten times larger, would be hard to contemplate without screaming. But they aren't, thank goodness! They are more afraid of us than we are of them. Truly scary garden critters are few and far between: poisonous snakes, yellow jackets, skunks, fire ants. Yet even these can be dispatched or avoided by a well-considered retreat.

Outside of the garden, and indeed sometimes in our hearts, there are bigger terrors lurking. Fear of illness and death, financial disaster, failures at work . . . . And unlike our garden frights, these are difficult to dispel and often difficult to name. Sometimes they are expressed only as a vague dread or free-floating anxiety and not clearly tied to any one thing.

Remember David's words in this verse and allay the fears that get in the way of living full lives. "You will not fear" because the Lord God is your salvation.

I will love thee, O LORD, my strength.
The LORD is my rock, and my fortress,
and my deliverer; my God,
my strength, in whom I will trust;
my buckler, and the horn of my salvation,
and my high tower.

PSALM 18:1–2 KJV

God Will Not Stretch Us
Beyond Our Capabilities

For he knows how we were made;
he remembers that we are dust.

PSALM 103:14 NRSV

∞

The words "ashes to ashes, dust to dust" are often part of the Christian graveside funeral service. They are especially poignant to the gardener. We work the soil and try to bring forth life from it. Yet even when all our plants are doing well—when the flowers have never looked more beautiful—in the back of our minds is the knowledge that it is all fleeting. We know their moment in the sun is only a matter of months. Come fall it will all be plowed under and the garden will be empty again.

Those dahlias that take our breath away and which seem so strong and vibrant in the sun are only here for an instant. We know their limitations. We want to encourage them. We want them to be the best they can be and give them what they need.

—————

We are God's creations. You can be confident that the trial you are currently facing will not overwhelm you, because God will give you the measure of faith He knows you need to endure.

I trust in your love.
My heart is happy because you saved me.
I sing to the LORD
because he has taken care of me.

PSALM 13:5–6 NCV

As for man, his days are like grass;
As a flower of the field, so he flourishes.
For the wind passes over it, and it is gone,
And its place remembers it no more.
But the mercy of the LORD is from everlasting to everlasting
On those who fear Him.

PSALM 103:15–17 NKJV

He is merciful and tender toward those
who don't deserve it;
he is slow to get angry
and full of kindness and love.

PSALM 103:8 TLB

Each day that we live,
he provides for our needs
and gives us the strength
of a young eagle.

PSALM 103:5 CEV

Nothing Is Impossible with God

He turns a desert into pools of water,
a parched land into springs of water.

PSALM 107:35 NRSV

∽

In Mexico there is a folk art form called the *milagro* cross. It is popular among rural people who live simply and close to the land, and for whom faith and religious observance are central to their lives. Literally translated, it means "miracle cross." Essentially, it is a simple crucifix made of wood to which individuals attach mementos of the various miracles God has worked in their lives. It's a kind of physical record for all to see of specific instances when God has helped them out of situations they thought were impossible.

Most often, these crosses are crowded with many pieces of gold and silver, representing an astounding number of times God saw fit to intervene in these poor peasants' lives. They are moving testimonies to the profound faith these agricultural people have in Christ. They expect and know He will answer them in times of trouble.

Faith in God moves mountains. Surely He can handle your troubles, no matter how dreadful and inevitable they may seem. Always remember to pray in faith and watch as God answers.

In my distress I prayed to the Lord,
and he answered me and rescued me.
He is for me! How can I be afraid?
What can mere man do to me?

PSALM 118:5–6 TLB

BE PATIENT AS GOD WORKS HIS WILL

I believe that I shall see the
goodness of the LORD
in the land of the living.

PSALM 27:13 NRSV

‿

While we are gardening, especially when we are doing simple, repetitive tasks like weeding or hoeing, we sometimes daydream and ruminate. In fact, it is one of the great pleasures of gardening that the mind relaxes and wanders. It's as if logic takes a little holiday and we ponder our wishes, hopes, and dreams unencumbered by grim reality. Thoughts of that little cottage on the beach we've wanted but can't afford help us pass the time as we lop dead blossoms off the roses. Or fond memories of our son's graduation from college sneak up on us: We can still picture him in gown and mortarboard as we rip the dandelions out of the daisy bed.

Actually, as we are going through the motions of some tedious task and contemplating our dreams, they begin to seem increasingly more achievable.

Our dreams are achievable in God's hands. Faith beats the odds every time. No matter that logic or reason say, "No way." In God's time and way, He will answer us.

Wait for the Lord;
Be strong, and let your
heart take courage;
Yes, wait for the Lord.
Psalm 27:14 NAS

I look up to the mountains;
does my strength come from mountains?
No, my strength comes from God,
who made heaven, and earth, and mountains.
Psalm 121:1 The Message

GOD IS MERCIFUL TO THE FAITHFUL

For you, O Lord, are good and forgiving,
abounding in steadfast love to
all who call on you.

PSALM 86:5 NRSV

◦∞◦

We all make mistakes because we all have weaknesses. And ever since Adam and Eve in their garden, we've had to fight our natural tendency to sin.

Granted, it is hard to commit a serious sin while gardening unless we go after someone with a hoe! But it *is* a good time to reflect on our previous trespasses. After all, only you, the plants, and God are listening. The "big ones" we've probably already talked to Him about many times. But the "littler ones," like showing a lack of charity to an irksome neighbor, gossiping about an acquaintance, or fibbing to get out of an obligation we really should have fulfilled, also deserve confession and repentance. Gardening is a good time to confront the issues and ask forgiveness.

———◦———

We are God's children, and when we sin, we sin against our heavenly Father. Use your quiet time to ask for His forgiveness and the strength to turn away from temptation.

As for me, I said, "O LORD,
be gracious to me;
Heal my soul, for I
have sinned against
Thee."
PSALM 41:4 NAS

For I know my transgressions,
and my sin is always before me.
Against you, you only, have I sinned
and done what is evil in your sight,
so that you are proved right when you speak
and justified when you judge.
PSALM 51:3–4 NIV

Our terrible sins get us down,
but you forgive us.
PSALM 65:3 CEV

Help us, God of our salvation!
Help us for the honor of your name.
Oh, save us and forgive our sins.
PSALM 79:9 TLB

GOD WILL DELIVER US THROUGH TOUGH TIMES

My days are like a shadow that declineth;
and I am withered like grass.
But thou, O LORD, shalt endure for ever;
and thy remembrance unto all generations.

PSALM 102:11–12 KJV

God never promised us a rose garden.
Underlying all of His promises to us is a
keen awareness of how difficult life can
be, even for the blessed. Life is a series
of defining moments of tough decisions, and refining fires of difficult
situations. At each juncture we have to
turn to our faith and hope in God to get
us safely through. He has provided us
with what we need, and the rest is up to
us. We are pilgrims as much as we are happy
gardeners. There will be troubles in our journey. Of this we can be
sure.

We will have spiritual droughts. We will have times when we feel
so down that we don't know which way is up. It will seem as if God
has vanished from our lives—or as if He doesn't exist at all, that
maybe it's all just a fairy tale.

When all of the lights go out and we feel utterly alone, we must
remember that this is life and that God is there, despite our inability
to see Him, in the midst of our troubles.

You have purified us with fire, O Lord,
like silver in a crucible. You captured us
in your net and laid great burdens on our backs.
You sent troops to ride across our broken bodies.
We went through fire and flood.
But in the end, you brought us
into wealth and great abundance.

PSALM 66:10-12 TLB

You made me suffer a lot,
but you will bring me
back from this deep pit
and give me new life.
You will make me truly great
and take my sorrow away.

PSALM 71:20-21 CEV

Your kingdom is built on what is right and fair.
Love and truth are in all you do.

PSALM 89:14 NCV

Blessed is the man whom thou chastenest, O LORD,
and teachest him out of thy law;
That thou mayest give him rest from the days of adversity,
until the pit be digged for the wicked.

PSALM 94:12-13 KJV

GOD PRESERVES ALL WHO LOVE HIM

You show me the path of life.
In your presence there is fullness of joy;
in your right hand are pleasures forevermore.

PSALM 16:11 NRSV

༑

As gardeners, we often take inspiration from other gardens, like the beautifully designed and maintained gardens we see in magazines. The spectacular public gardens such as the New York Botanical Gardens, Calloway Gardens in Georgia, the gardens at Williamsburg and Mount Vernon are all feasts to our gardeners' eyes.

They are so perfectly planned and executed, we remember the shortcomings of our own gardens. We make mental lists of things we'd like to change and improve when we return home. We get ideas for new plants and themes we can't wait to try out. These other gardens are marvels to behold and fill us with energy and enthusiasm we are eager to unleash on our own bit of paradise.

Our minds crowd with details we have overlooked—borders that need work, proper irrigation of plantings, the right plants for shady spots in the garden.

In life, the Lord is our example and inspiration. If we look to Him for direction in all things, we will prosper and become a thing of beauty in His eyes.

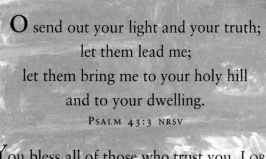

O send out your light and your truth;
let them lead me;
let them bring me to your holy hill
and to your dwelling.
PSALM 43:3 NRSV

You bless all of those who trust you, LORD,
and refuse to worship idols or follow false gods.
You, LORD God, have done many wonderful things,
and you have planned marvelous things for us.
No one is like you!
I would never be able to tell all you have done.
PSALM 40:4–5 CEV

As for me, I will behold thy face in righteousness:
I shall be satisfied, when I awake, with thy likeness.
PSALM 17:15 KJV

GOD'S GOODNESS SATISFIES THE LONGING AND HUNGRY SOUL

*For he satisfies the thirsty,
and the hungry he fills with good things.*

PSALM 107:9 NRSV

More than once gardeners have remarked that their flowers seem to have human faces. This metaphor has found its way into many poems. It's a sweet notion, particularly when we are caring for them, watering and feeding them, to think of these lovely blossoms as tiny people we are tending to, even when we know the idea is only fanciful.

Deep within us, as children of God, we have a need to shower love and care on living things. It is an impulse as natural as any other we have and cannot be denied. A sense of peace comes to us as we minister to others; there is no feeling more satisfying. The sight of a vulnerable man, animal, or plant brings forth in us a genuine response of love and a need to care. It actually diminishes us if we are, for some reason, unable to answer that need with action.

We were made in God's image and likeness. He is the model for our behavior, and in showing care and love for His creation we are being true to Him, our caring heavenly Father.

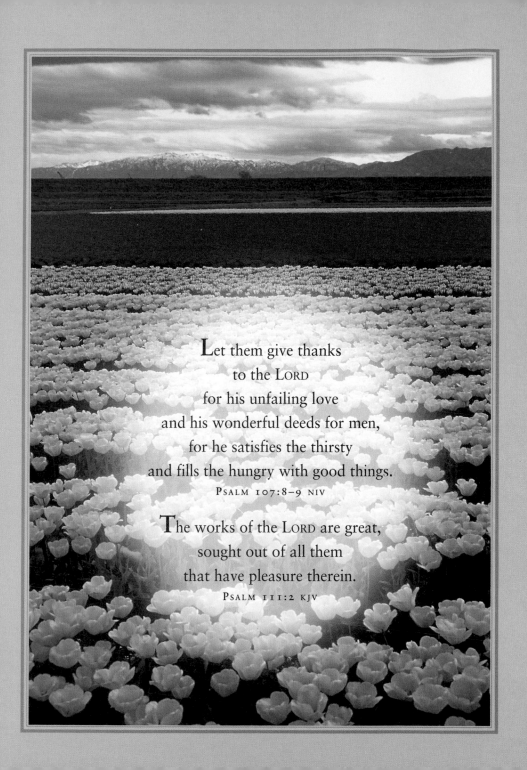

Let them give thanks
to the LORD
for his unfailing love
and his wonderful deeds for men,
for he satisfies the thirsty
and fills the hungry with good things.

PSALM 107:8–9 NIV

The works of the LORD are great,
sought out of all them
that have pleasure therein.

PSALM 111:2 KJV

POWER OF GOD

The voice of the LORD is over the waters;
the God of glory thunders,
the LORD, over mighty waters.

PSALM 29:3 NRSV

Gardeners are acquainted with the small beginnings of life. When we hear the phrase "the miracle of life," we think immediately of seeds, those unlikely looking tiny husks containing the future flower, vegetable, or tree. Inasmuch as we deal with, hold, manipulate, bury, fertilize, and water them, we are still astonished when they break open and mature into life forms both beautiful and grand.

Seed parables and metaphors abound in the Bible. The mustard seed, the seeds that fall on stony ground, Abraham's seed—seed is the universal biblical code word for great things from apparently insignificant beginnings. They are a microcosm of the universe, for coiled within them is everything God intended them to be, down to the color of the flower and the length of the petals. The complex power it takes to render the whole of a mighty oak into an acorn is enough to boggle the mind.

Imagine the possibilities in our lives if we are tapped into that same power as the source of our strength. Do we call on the Lord daily for help in developing our full potential?

But as for me, I will sing about your power.
I will shout with joy each morning
because of your unfailing love.
For you have been my refuge,
a place of safety in the day of distress.
PSALM 59:16 NLT

God's Abundant Peace

But the meek shall inherit the land,
and delight themselves in abundant prosperity.

PSALM 37:11 NRSV

∽

Meek? Like the scared little mice we find in the pantry? Like the rabbits that flee from us when they see us coming? What is this "meek" business? If we were meek in going about our gardening chores, not much would get done and we wouldn't have much of a garden. Imagine timidly weeding, passively watering, fearfully planting seeds. There is no place for meekness in a gardener's lexicon.

But the psalmist didn't use the word *meek* in the same way we do today. He meant meek in the presence of the Lord; he meant patient and steadfast in our observance of the Lord's commandments; he meant harboring no resentments, but accepting what God sends us. We are right in being meek before God; He is indeed infinitely more powerful than we are, and we are nothing without Him.

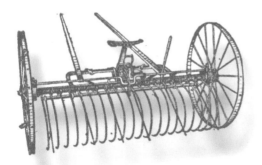

Let us always be meek in the biblical sense with respect to our Lord. As He promised, He will reward us with the abundance of His blessings.

The humble shall see their God
at work for them.
No wonder they will be so glad!
All who seek for God shall live in joy.

PSALM 69:32 TLB

You crown the year with a bountiful harvest;
even the hard pathways overflow with
abundance.
The wilderness becomes a lush pasture,
and the hillsides blossom with joy.
The meadows are clothed with flocks of sheep,
and the valleys are carpeted with grain.
They all shout and sing for joy!

PSALM 65:11–13 NLT

GOD'S MIRACULOUS PROVISIONS

He split rocks open in the wilderness,
and gave them drink abundantly
as from the deep.

PSALM 78:15 NRSV

❧

How many times have we said as gardeners, "It's hopeless"?
A stand of corn is flattened by hail, tulip leaves are crushed by a
careless foot, seeds refuse to sprout. These things don't happen often,
but they happen enough so that we are familiar with lost causes and
the disappointment they bring. Sometimes, though,
the outcome surprises us. Plants that were
given up for dead turn green and
straighten up. Unexpectedly, July
1, our long forgotten crocuses
finally push through the soil.
Late November, last year's
poinsettias, abandoned in a dark
corner of the garage, grow leaves
and buds. *It's a miracle,* we think.
In our own lives, God knows
when we need divine help. He knows
exactly what we need, how much we need
to flourish, and the best time to provide the miracle of His power.

⸻

We need to be open to God's hand and listen to His Word.
Then our hearts are always prepared for His blessings and we don't
limit His power in our lives.

Sing to the LORD a new song,
because he has done miracles.
By his right hand and holy arm
he has won the victory.

PSALM 98:1 NCV

Trust the LORD and his mighty power.
Remember his miracles and all his wonders
and his fair decisions.

PSALM 105:4-5 CEV

GOD'S GOODNESS

The LORD is truthful; he can be trusted.
He loves justice and fairness,
and he is kind to everyone everywhere on earth.

PSALM 33:4–5 CEV

A woman in northern Florida dreams of spring all through the rainy cold days of winter. She spends her time hatching plans for the most splendid garden she has ever had. She analyzes last year's garden and how to improve it. Because she has gone through this process for many years, she knows exactly what pests and weather conditions she is going to have to contend with month by month.

Because of her experience, every growing season she dreads July. July is days of unrelenting hot weather and weeds. July is little rainfall. July is what inevitably comes after all the plants have come up and she has gotten over the initial delight of being a "new mother." July is just plain work. Somehow she will get through it though because she is devoted.

God's goodness flows to those who hang in there. When God's people stick to the plan, they are righteous and just and He in return repays them with His steadfast love.

The good man does not escape all troubles—
he has them too. But the Lord helps him
in each and every one.

PSALM 34:19 TLB

The steps of a good man
are ordered by the LORD:
and he delighteth in his way.
Though he fall, he shall not be utterly cast down:
for the LORD upholdeth him with his hand.

PSALM 37:23–24 KJV

I, the LORD, am your God,
who brought you out of Egypt.
Open your mouth and I will feed you.

PSALM 81:10 NCV

CALLED BY GOD TO SEEK HIS FACE ALL DAY

The mighty one, God the LORD,
speaks and summons the earth
from the rising of the sun to its setting.

PSALM 50:1 NRSV

❧

An orchard offers us many delights. The trees are stately with their branches reaching to the sky. At first, fragrant flowers appear, which then drop and drift across the ground. They are then followed by fruits in every spot that had produced a flower. Finally, the fruits swell and ripen and fall to the ground where they lie scattered like blessings from the tree. A lady we know has a pear orchard and observes this cycle every year. She also raises miniature horses and has a big, galumphing dog. Each year the animals watch the trees because they have learned to love pears. When the fruit is ripe they are pesky begging for it. If pears fall to the ground, the dog teases the horses with them. The tiny horses press against the fence until the woman throws them some of the sweet, ripe fruit.

We, like ripening fruit, have to wait patiently for God to work His will in our lives. His creation illustrates His timing to mature us to perfection in Him, and circumstances help show us His path and blessings along the journey.

I have been young, and now am old;
yet have I not seen the righteous forsaken,
nor his seed begging bread.
He is ever merciful, and lendeth; and his seed is blessed.
Depart from evil, and do good; and dwell for evermore.
For the LORD loveth judgment,
and forsaketh not his saints.

PSALM 37:25–28 KJV

Honor and majesty are before Him;
Strength and beauty are in His sanctuary.

PSALM 96:6 NKJV

TRUTH AND RIGHTEOUSNESS, THE FRUIT OF WALKING WITH GOD

*Faithfulness will spring up from the ground,
and righteousness will look down from the sky.*

PSALM 85:11 NRSV

∽

Ladybugs, as every gardener knows, are supposed to be signs of good fortune. Unlike the appearance of other insects, they make a gardener smile. The appearance of ladybugs in a garden means it's a happy, prosperous place and that the soil and conditions for growing are good. Ladybugs don't show up just anywhere. They have high standards indeed. Hence the name *lady*, maybe. These tiny red insects, the size of a small pea with little black dots on their backs, accent flower petals and leaves. The sun glints off their backs, and they flutter from one perch to the next, eating undesirable insects and conveying a spirit of contentment throughout their surroundings.

Some gardening catalogs even offer ladybugs for sale. But like the lovely ladies they are, if they don't like their destination, they pack up and leave!

———

Watch for signs of God's blessings all around you today and, like our speckled insect friends, be diligent to live a life of faithfulness so that your life, too, can be a source of blessing to your loved ones.

O LORD of hosts,
How blessed is the man
who trusts in Thee!
PSALM 84:12 NAS

Righteousness and justice are the
foundation of your throne;
love and faithfulness go before you.
Blessed are those who have learned to acclaim you,
who walk in the light of your presence, O LORD.
They rejoice in your name all day long;
they exult in your righteousness.
PSALM 89:14–16 NIV

But I will never stop loving him,
nor let my promise to him fail.
No, I will not break my covenant;
I will not take back a single word I said.
PSALM 89:33–34 NLT

GOD CAN BE TRUSTED TO SUPPLY OUR NEEDS

He rained down on them manna to eat,
and gave them the grain of heaven.

PSALM 78:24 NRSV

∽

Damping-off is the bane of the energetic, not to say optimistic, gardener who plants seeds in containers in late winter. Working under fluorescent lights, she prepares just the right soil mixture in the small wells that will host each seed. Then gently, after straining her eyes on the small print on the back of the packet, she sets each seed at just the right depth.

Weeks go by and nothing happens. She checks the seed packets for reassurance. She checks the thermometer in the room. She stares at the containers and even imagines she sees microscopic points of green poking through the soil. Then one day tendrils do show up, quickly followed by the appearance of two fully formed leaves. But days later, on her daily visit, she finds the tiny plants drooped over in a faint. Nothing she does will revive them. *Damping-off* is the sudden infant death syndrome of the greenhouse.

───────

God is the only source of true sustenance. No matter the extent of our expertise, diligence, wisdom, or strength in life, it will never be enough without Him.

When they reach Dry Valley,
springs start flowing,
and the autumn rain fills it
with pools of water.
Your people grow stronger,
and you, the God of gods,
will be seen in Zion.

PSALM 84:6–7 CEV

For thou art the glory of their strength:
and in thy favour our horn shall be exalted.
For the LORD is our defence;
and the Holy One of Israel is our king.

PSALM 89:17–18 KJV

The LORD himself watches over you!
The LORD stands beside you as your protective shade.
The sun will not hurt you by day,
nor the moon at night.
The LORD keeps you from all evil
and preserves your life.

PSALM 121:5–7 NLT

Satisfied with God's Mercy

*Satisfy us in the morning with your steadfast love,
so that we may rejoice and be glad all our days.*

Psalm 90:14 NRSV

∞

Gardening has rituals that are as much a part of the pleasure of the activity as planting and watching things grow. For instance, going over the seed catalogs in the dead of winter by the fire. Visiting the nurseries in early spring and appraising their beds of plants and bushes. Getting out the old rubber gardening boots to see if they'll do for yet another year. Measuring off the garden and deciding what is going to go where. Sharing plans with other gardeners and asking for their opinion. These are all part of the experience.

As we observe these rituals anew, we know deep down that we are once more shaking off the winter doldrums and reentering the cycle of life. They are quiet affirmations that life indeed goes on and that we are part of it. The sweet repetition of these annual activities has a sacramental feel to it and rekindles joy in our hearts.

Greet each morning by seeking God first. Make this quiet time the most important ritual of the day. Recommit yourself to Him, placing yourself in His mercy.

Teach us how short our lives really are
so that we may be wise.

Psalm 90:12 NCV

Rejoice in the Lord

Let the heavens be glad, the earth rejoice;
let the vastness of the roaring seas
demonstrate his glory.

PSALM 96:11 TLB

∾

Have you ever met an unhappy gardener? People who are cantankerous and dismal about life generally don't take up gardening. If they do, and stick with it, subtle transformations begin to take place, and before they know it their smile muscles are aching.

Certainly gardening, like life, has its small frustrations and big failures. Every gardener has her list of disappointments. The year she sprayed defoliant rather than insect spray on the roses. The time she set out 250 bulbs at her property line and the water company decided that was where they needed to lay new pipe. But she learns with each experience and goes on. Gardening is a process. The point is not in the result, although when everything turns out well it's great. The point is in the doing. It is the continuous expression of faith in the sacredness of life.

God wants us to be happy in this miracle of life He has given us. He wants us to celebrate the special joys each new day brings.

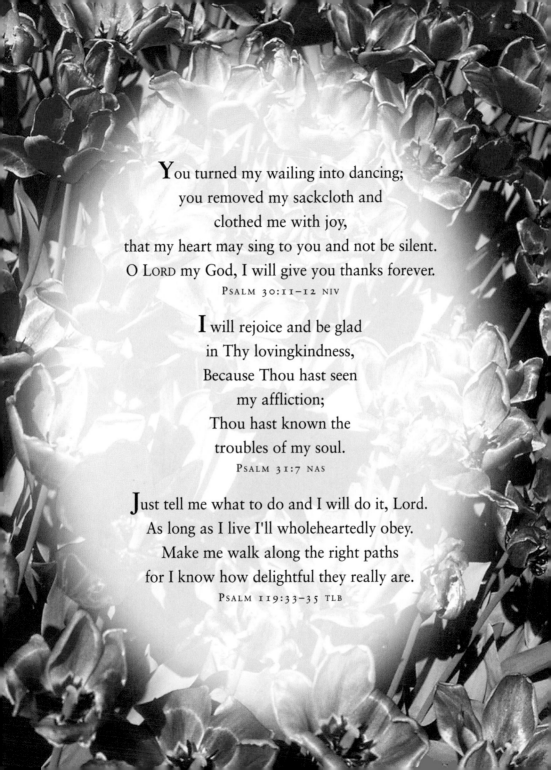

You turned my wailing into dancing;
you removed my sackcloth and
clothed me with joy,
that my heart may sing to you and not be silent.
O LORD my God, I will give you thanks forever.

<small>PSALM 30:11–12 NIV</small>

I will rejoice and be glad
in Thy lovingkindness,
Because Thou hast seen
my affliction;
Thou hast known the
troubles of my soul.

<small>PSALM 31:7 NAS</small>

Just tell me what to do and I will do it, Lord.
As long as I live I'll wholeheartedly obey.
Make me walk along the right paths
for I know how delightful they really are.

<small>PSALM 119:33–35 TLB</small>

GOD LOVINGLY CARES FOR HIS CREATION

He makes grass grow for the cattle,
and plants for man to cultivate —
bringing forth food from the earth.

PSALM 104:14 NIV

One of the favorite memories of a certain gardener involves sugar snap peas. When his children were very young, he wanted to introduce them to the joys of gardening. They planted seeds for various things, but the peas came up first and were the first to bear. The kids loved eating them right off the vine in the garden. The sight of his three young children, now college graduates, eating those sugar snap peas in their first garden has stayed with him over the years. You can't mention *peas* in his presence without his bringing it up. For him it is a moving image of what life is all about: God's fruitfulness, abundance, and blessings. Seeing his young children reaping the bounty of what they had sown made this one of the happiest moments of his life.

We have moments when we see clearly how kind God is to us. When His stupendous miracle of life and its many blessings suddenly come into sharp focus, treasure them.

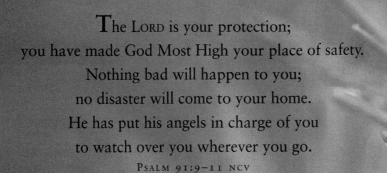

The LORD is your protection;
you have made God Most High your place of safety.
Nothing bad will happen to you;
no disaster will come to your home.
He has put his angels in charge of you
to watch over you wherever you go.

PSALM 91:9–11 NCV

The LORD has mercy on those who respect him,
as a father has mercy on his children.

PSALM 103:13 NCV

PRAYER FOR BLESSINGS

Deal bountifully with your servant,
so that I may live and observe your word.

PSALM 119:17 NRSV

Over time, gardeners accumulate large storehouses of experience from which they can draw to deal with their present garden. It's a wonderful thing that as the seasons and years pile up atop one another they provide harvests of wisdom useful for subsequent gardens. This ensures that each mistake or success is not ephemeral, but will find its way into the new year and contribute to the current garden's success. Furthermore, to gardeners there is no Armageddon or rapture. Life, enriched by the past, goes on, improved by historical defeats and victories.

As the gardener's past experience prepares and inspires her to start all over again each new spring, so also God brings remembrance of previous times of answered prayers and blessings to encourage and equip us to be diligent in our love and service today.

As we learn to walk with the Lord, we build up treasured memories of His tender mercies in our lives. Armed with these memories, we are sustained and encouraged and invigorated in our faith.

I truly believe
I will live to see the LORD's goodness.
Wait for the LORD's help.
Be strong and brave,
and wait for the LORD's help.

PSALM 27:13–14 NCV

WAIT PATIENTLY ON THE LORD

I waited patiently for the LORD;
he inclined to me and heard my cry.

PSALM 40:1 NRSV

A woman, displeased by the quality of grass seed she had purchased from the local farmer's co-op, called to complain. "It never came up," she said, as she explained that she had done everything right and had never had any trouble with grass seed before.

The clerk told her to "take a number and get in line." They'd had numerous complaints about this year's grass seed.

The woman thought of the brown patches and bare spots on her lawn and the hours spent sowing seed. It was nearly July. She had prepared the ground ahead of time, before she had sown the seed. Then she had covered it with straw and watered it carefully. She could still feel the bugs in her face and the dust in her hair. It was too late to get a good turf going this year.

We face setbacks when no one, not even God, seems to care. With Him you'll never have to "get in line." The truth is, He is the only One who does care and will hear our every prayer, answering in His perfect timing.

Show me your ways, O Lord,
teach me your paths;
guide me in your truth and teach me,
for you are God my Savior,
and my hope is in you all day long.

PSALM 25:4 NIV

ALL CREATION PRAISES GOD

Let them praise the name of the LORD,
for his name alone is exalted;
his glory is above earth and heaven.

PSALM 148:13 NRSV

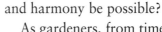

There is a famous early American painting entitled *Peaceable Kingdom*. In it the wolf lies down with the lamb and a little girl embraces a huge grizzly bear. Indians talk peacefully with men in three-cornered hats, and a cow consorts with a lion as if they were friends. It is a wonderfully peaceful scene inspired by Isaiah's prophecy of peace to come (Isaiah 11:6–9). God's presence and influence are everywhere in the scene. How else could this miracle of peace

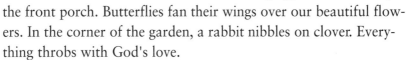

and harmony be possible?

As gardeners, from time to time, we catch glimpses of this rare harmony in nature. On a certain fine day outdoors, everything alive seems to be happy and thriving. The birds are singing, the cat is asleep on the front porch. Butterflies fan their wings over our beautiful flowers. In the corner of the garden, a rabbit nibbles on clover. Everything throbs with God's love.

Our debt to God is to create as many of these harmonious moments as we can. We can do this by exalting His name in the glorious world He has given each of us to garden.

I pray that the LORD will let your family
and your descendants always grow strong.
May the LORD who created the heavens and the earth
give you his blessing.

PSALM 115:14–15 CEV

I will sing of the tender mercies of the LORD forever!
Young and old will hear of your faithfulness.
Your unfailing love will last forever.
Your faithfulness is as enduring as the heavens.

PSALM 89:1–2 NLT

This and other books in the Psalms Gift Edition™ series are available from your local bookstore.

Lighthouse Psalms

Garden Psalms

Love Psalms

If you have enjoyed this book, or if it has impacted your life, we would like to hear from you. Please contact us at:

Honor Books
Department E
P.O. Box 55388
Tulsa, Oklahoma 74155

Or by e-mail at info@honorbooks.com